Life thro

eyes

Katherine Bailey

BookLeaf
Publishing

India | USA | UK

Life through my eyes © 2024 Katherine
Bailey

All rights reserved.

No part of this publication may be
reproduced, stored in a retrieval system, or
transmitted, in any form or by any means,
electronic, mechanical, photocopying,
recording or otherwise, without the prior
written permission of the presenters.

Katherine Bailey asserts the moral right to
be identified as author of this work.

Presentation by *BookLeaf Publishing*

Web: www.bookleafpub.com

E-mail: info@bookleafpub.com

ISBN: 9789358313505

First edition 2024

DEDICATION

These poems are dedicated to anyone &
everyone who is struggling with their health. I
hope you can relate to some of these, and it
brings you comfort, confidence, and
compassion.

ACKNOWLEDGEMENT

Most importantly, thank you to my family. I wouldn't be here today without you. You have given up your life to make mine the best it can be, and you couldn't have done a better job.
Thank you to the strangers that I have met as a result of my health and are now my best friends - you're truly my greatest inspirations.
Thank you to my husband, Sam, for being my absolute rock. I love you with all my heart and I always will.

Ultimately, thank you to the NHS for saving my life on more than just a couple of occasions. We don't realise just how lucky we are.

PREFACE

Hi all, and thank you for choosing to read my collection of poems.

This is in fact my first ever attempt at poem writing, so I've experimented with a variety of forms and techniques for both your benefit, but mine as well!

I'm 27 & I now live in Worthing despite being born and growing up in Sidcup, Kent. I live with my husband - Sam - who I married just 6 months before writing this, and we love it here by the sea.

As previously mentioned, we are both chronically ill and rely on carers to help us live a 'normal' life, but are lucky enough to have the most lovely, supportive team of carers around us; to provide us with the help we need to live our lives together as we wish.

My main condition is Ehlers-Danlos Syndrome. Secondary to this is Postural Orthostatic Tachycardia Syndrome (PoTS), Mast Cell Activation Disorder (MCAD), Gastroparesis/Intestinal Dysmotility & Bladder

Dysfunction, and Sam has a diagnosis of Duchenne Muscular Dystrophy.

Although you wouldn't believe it (even I don't at times!), but I am more than the multiple conditions that I've been diagnosed with, my ever-growing list of allergies, the tubes and lines and scars in and on my body, and the prescription upon prescription of medication that my body rattles with...

My first blog – 'Sixteen, Swollen & Spontaneous Anaphylaxis' – was started around the beginning of 2013; the intention of it being a diary/journal to regularly update everyone on my health. Not only that, but at that time I was still so far from any diagnosis, my blog served as an accurate 'timeline' for me to accurately track symptoms, hospital appointments, admissions, treatments, and my general wellbeing overall.

As time went by and with the changes in my health, I started a completely different blog entirely: 'Life through my eyes'; this was once I had been diagnosed, and was intended for posts on a broader spectrum to illness/disability, when I did a lot of fundraising and charity work (mostly from my hospital bed!) and one that I hoped that readers found a lot more open and honest too.

I now have a blog with Sam - 'our not so straightforward relationship' - which includes a range of diary entries, posts, photos, information, charities, fundraising, competitions, and support for those who need it.

Other than that, I am working towards pacing and learning what I can do, without over-exerting my body and suffering after. I am studying for a degree in Law (via distance learning, organised and supported by Kent Law School), so whether it be working towards that (doing the impossible amount of reading per week!), visiting family, going out socially with my friends, spending time with Sam ticking things off of our bucket list, or having a PJ day at home, I am learning to take each day as it comes and deal with what each day throws at me in the best way I can.

Welcome along this journey with me!

My Chronic Illness Journey

My broken body started to break
When I was aged just 9,
a dislocated knee, a lazy eye,
All we thought would heal just fine.

Aged 16 my health deteriorated
And nobody knew just why,
I wasn't responding to treatment,
But I'd still continue to try.

It began with allergies and anaphylaxis,
Many of the triggers unknown,
So I now have a tracheostomy,
And carers so I'm never alone.

It then started to affect my stomach,
Agony i just couldn't take,
A feeding tube was inserted,
As eating I could no longer partake

My joints were the next to cause problems,
It's hard to describe the pain,
But relocating a joint dislocation,
Is by far the best skill to gain!

Afterwards came the seizures,
Worsened by infection and stress,
Whether absence or tonic clonic,
Every day they cause some distress.

Also given up is my bladder,
Retention leaves me in tears,
I'm now an expert in catheters,
Having lived with a Suprapubic for years.

For years we had no answers,
No idea of what was wrong,
How these symptoms were connected,
And why they were lasting so long.

It's only when I was hospitalised
That I started to join the dots,
A diagnosis of Ehlers-Danlos,
Led also to a diagnosis of PoTS*

This continued like dominoes,
Mast Cell** was next to be found,
A multitude of illnesses,
Which have left me wheelchair-bound.

Every day I mourn for a 'normal life',
the future I had planned to a tee,
But in the end I have come to accept,
that such a life just wasn't for me.

I'm thankful for the positives,
For where my conditions have made me thrive,
But most importantly, against all odds,
I'm here; I'm still alive!

*Postural Orthostatic Tachycardia Syndrome

**Mast Cell Activation Disorder

Diagnosis

Imagine at the tender age of 16,
After being 'well' for your whole life,
To suddenly develop a mystery illness,
Calling an ambulance on a regular basis,
Hoping that you'll get to the hospital on time.

Imagine, being thrown into the world of adult
medicine,
Admitted to hospital for days, weeks, months at
a time,
And still not knowing what's wrong,
But just knowing that the future,
Will never look the same again.

Imagine, at the age of 18, you've deteriorated so
dramatically
That the safest place for you is intensive care,
Where the sickest people of the hospital are
looked after.
Most in a coma, their families not knowing if
they're going to live or die,
And having to witness that.

Imagine, after fighting the hardest battle of your
life,

Just to be told that it's all in your head,
That you're making it up,
And the only referral I needed, was to see a
gastroenterologist.

Imagine, after being told you're a fraud,
That you have to walk into another appointment,
Expecting the worst (from experience),
But actually to coincidentally see an experienced
professor,
And to leave the consultation room with a
diagnosis!

You cannot imagine, the emotions that I felt
And it's strange to say,
That I was overjoyed to have a name; a
diagnosis
But it meant no more being doubted,
Or assumed to have a mental health problem to
explain my symptoms.

Imagine, after a 3 hour appointment,
To be reunited with my dad in the waiting room,
To be able to tell him that I know what is wrong,
That finally we have help, referrals, a treatment
plan,
All we could do is burst into tears.

Reminiscing

Do not feel angry, when you think back to the
day,
That you had bundles of energy, that you could
run, laugh and play.
You appeared healthy as a child; nothing to
indicate any different,
Born into the world, as an innocent infant.

Do not feel sad, that you did not realise before,
That your feeling of 'normality', was in fact a
lot more.
It's of no fault of your own, that you suddenly
became sick,
The future is unknown, and impossible to
predict.

Do not feel embarrassed, about the person you
are now,
The illnesses that you have do not define you
anyhow,
The tubes and lines that are in your body, the
scars that you may bear,
Simply show your strength and fight to live; for
that you should not care.

Do not feel guilty, for the way that you may feel,
It's okay not to be okay, it's okay to just be real,
Do not compare others to what you're going
through yourself,
Because the reality isn't that simple when it
comes down to your health.

Do not feel frustrated, that you can't go back in
time,
Of course - to live a life of health - would be
nothing but sublime,
'Hindsight is a wonderful thing', they say - but
there's nothing you can do,
But embrace the illness that you're now living
with,
As time won't wait for you.

Do not feel hurt when looking back at your
childhood free from fear,
Your health was stolen from you overnight, and
destroyed within a year,
Remember all you've learnt and gained; just
from illness alone,
And be thankful for the positives that in a
decade, you have grown.

Everything happens for a reason

Although it may not be immediately apparent,
I do believe that 'everything happens for a
reason'.
I do believe there was a reason I have this illness
to battle,
It's just yet to become clear.

And it's because of the circumstances with my
health,
That I've seen incredible places,
Met inspiring people,
and done things I never would have before.

I have an incredible family, amazing friends, and
supportive carers,
who provide more support than I could put into
words,
so although my future isn't panning out the way
I thought it would,
I still have a future regardless, and for that, I am
grateful.

Feeling left behind

Imagine just reaching the age, where you have
more independence and freedom,
and the chance to gain more life experience,
Then imagine having it snatched from you in
front of your eyes.

The feeling of being 'left behind', as you see the
friends you've grown up with,
transition from childhood into adulthood,
from school to college/sixth form and university;
graduating and venturing out in the world,
It's bitter-sweet, sometimes I'm envious to be
honest.

Going from living with their parents to
becoming parents,
Just at a time that my life was interrupted,
My plans stopped in their tracks by a mystery
illness,
Which converted my blossoming career as a
high-flying lawyer to a long-term hospital
patient.

Every day, I'm no less told how 'strong' and 'brave' I am, despite in myself, not feeling strong or brave at all.
How I'm an 'inspiration' and a 'role model' to others battling with their health,
Of course though, these are all such lovely things to hear,
And in fact it's those compliments that keep me fighting, even on my worst days.

Now, I have deteriorated to the point of needing round the clock care from multiple trained carers/nurses,
I've been so lucky with the people who do care for me, some of my carers are my best friends too and have made memories that none of us will forget.
But above all, they care, they listen, we laugh,
And to a select few, who have been in the right place at the wrong time, I literally owe my life.

I've now come round to accept
that good health and quality of life,
Plus spending time with those who are important to you,
are what matters most above anything.
So don't forget to remind those that you love,
just how much you love them

Doubting Doctors

If you are unwell, but the doctor doesn't know
what's wrong,
It doesn't mean that it's nothing,
Or that you're making it up.
Or that you're imagining it.
Or that you should ignore it

It simply means that you need more help,
It needs more in depth knowledge.
More opinions.
More tests.
More scans.

But Doctor's don't like not knowing what's
wrong.
It's affects their profession.
Their career.
Their years of study.
Their ego.

So the diagnosis they make for a physical
illness,
Is often instead a psychological one.
Which is deflating.
Which is frustrating.

Which is incorrect.

The most important thing to remember,
Is to keep fighting for the right answer.
Only you know how you're feeling.
Only you know what's normal.
Only you know your body.

And I know when you're told to keep fighting,
It's beyond tiring, physically and mentally,
when you're unwell.
when you're weak.
when you're vulnerable.

You don't want to hear the medical jargon for
'nothing is wrong'
But sometimes, it's easier to accept it anyway
because
It's too much energy to fight back.
It's not worth arguing.
It's not going to change anything.

But when all's said and done, it's only you who
is suffering.
Because once the doctor has finished their shift,
They're tired, but happy.
They're going home to their family.
They're not thinking of their patients.

So ultimately, in the end, it's down to you.
It may be hard now, but it'll be worth it.
With the right treatment.
With the right care.
With the the right diagnosis.

Do you trust a single human being, who has no
knowledge about what's wrong,
to determine your diagnosis,
to determine your future,
to determine the rest of your life?

Dear Doctor

Dear Doctors,

I imagine, that in the same way
You can't imagine what it must feel like
To live with constant debilitating symptoms
That accompany the life-limiting illnesses that
we were dealt.
We can't imagine how difficult it must be to sort
out
The problems we present to you with.

Our 'normality' is different to that of a healthy
person
Our 'normal' incorporates our 'normal'
symptoms
Of pain, fatigue, nausea, faints,
And the myriad of other symptoms from which
we suffer.
So, "I'm fine" to us actually means
that we're suffering from our usual symptoms
That all have become our new 'normal'
- a 'normal' defined much differently
to how others would define it.

When it comes to those who think

That we are exaggerating our pain,
Our emotions, and our fatigue?
It's disheartening
That these people have chosen a career in care,
Yet they don't care
Or have been in the job for too long to care.

It's hard to ignore the doubts and accusations
Of 'putting on your illness'.
And we could (and do!) see hundreds and
hundreds of doctors
Who can clearly see, understand, and try to treat
our illness(es),
Yet it's the one or two doctors that don't believe
us
That stick in our heads and can
cause mental scars that never disappear.

Negative comments from healthcare
'professionals' – to tell you the truth – are so
unprofessional,
But relentless.
And after a while, you learn that you HAVE to
trust your own body.
You have to fight for tests and scans when you
know things aren't right.
You have to seek second opinions.
You have to do what you need to do to ensure
that you're listened to;

Because only we know how we feel.
We're experts in our own conditions.
We know what's normal and when something's wrong.
Nobody else understands our body like we do,
so we have to trust ourselves when something isn't right,
however many times we're told that nothing is wrong.

We're constantly reminded of our frailty, Our limits and our mortality in everything we do,
In every day that passes.
How do we cope? Well we don't have any other choice.
We have to cope. We can't just 'give up'.
We learn to live with our conditions
Because we have to,
But we never fully 'accept' it; we just learn to cope.

It's most likely the case that patients - like us - do scare you, as doctors.
And that's perfectly fine.
But do you not think that we're scared too?
Of each gruelling procedure, of each new doctor, of every new symptom, of our future?
I've already spoken about those who doubt us – with that experience comes fear.

We're scared too; yet we have and never have
had any choice over what our body throws at us
next.
You have far more choice in the matter than we
do,
but we have to put on a brave face and carry on
with each day, on behalf of all of us,
We're asking for you to do that too.

Many doctors don't seem to recognise
that we are sick of everything medical-related.
It rules our life, and we avoid hospitals at all
costs.
So when we present to you, it's because we need
help.
It's because we are experiencing symptoms
beyond our normal,
symptoms that aren't within our threshold and
have exceeded our limits of looking after
ourselves -
either because we haven't experienced the
symptoms before,
or they are much worse than we can cope with.
The hospital is the last place we want to be and
really is the last resort;
A life or death situation for many of us
so please don't question why we 'left it so late'
or if 'we think we can cope at home'.
We're scared,

We're vulnerable,
And we most certainly wouldn't be sitting in
front of you if we didn't need to be,
believe me.

Many doctors fail to realise that we, as patients,
would much rather
they admit that they aren't familiar with our
conditions,
that they haven't dealt with anyone in their
career so far as complex as us,
and they don't know how to help without input
from a more senior colleague.
We respect you far more for that,
than pretending you know what you're talking
about,
giving us medication that doesn't help,
and sending us home again,
knowing we will only return later with
worsening symptoms.
Most of the time, we know what is best,
you just need to trust us,
talk to us,
and listen to what we know we need.
We know you're not superhuman,
you're an emergency doctor with little
knowledge about hundreds of illnesses,
we don't expect you to be expert in the rarest,
most complex conditions we have.

We don't expect to walk out of the emergency
department with a cure to the incurable,
a diagnosis to the unknown,
or even a treatment to the untreatable.
But do you see now why we are scared of new
doctors?
It's not your fault that we are,
but the reason we ignore you is out of fear of
everything I've mentioned so far.
But most importantly,
of having to recall our history to you,
with the fear of not being believed.
As a general doctor, we're relieved if you've
even heard of our weird and wonderful diseases,
so to know nothing about them is far from
unusual for us,
and we just want to be listened to,
then you'll understand the reason we've
presented to you,
and what we require from you.
That's the key to ever building up a bond with
the chronically ill.

The last thing for you to resemble, is that the
majority of us with chronic illnesses aren't
horrible people
who are out to give doctors a hard time,

and we're sorry for the times we come across as ungrateful
It's not a personal thing,
we're just tired.
Living with a chronic illness that affects every part of your life is hard enough.
Having to fight for care, however, is so much harder.
So, please forgive us,
and know that deep down,
even when it doesn't seem like it, your work to us is invaluable.

We're just people who got dealt a poor hand when it comes to our health.
You're just people who chose a career to care for us,
diagnose and treat our medical problems,
and ultimately
I would like to think
try and make the lives of the chronically ill just a little bit better.
It must be frustrating when you can't 'fix us',
but we're not asking that of you, we're just asking for a bit of help in our worst times;
in our times of need.

Thank you for all you do,
For saving our lives over and over again.

We know your intentions are good.
We know you want the best for us,
and we know that you try and do what you can.
We are grateful for everything you do.
All the time you have compassion and empathy,
we will appreciate you.

Sincerely,

The Chronically Ill.

*In reply to 'A Letter to patients with Chronic
illness' - Dr Rob
https://www.medpagetoday.com/opinion/drrob/2
1266

Spoons

Early morning, my alarm starts to ring
I wonder what the day will bring

I'm already tired but anyway
I've got 12 new spoons to use today

I get myself up and out of bed
I'm pacing well; 11 spoons ahead

My meds are administered, all fifty of them
That in itself means I'm down to spoon 10

I meet my friend for a coffee in town
9 spoons left - that's another one down!

Brain fog hits, I drop to spoon 8,
I have an appointment and I'm already late!

I return home, and use all of my power,
Including spoon 7 just to have a shower

Sacrificing spoon 6 I have to bear,
I can't even remember when I last washed my
hair!

Two spoons for the next part; one for each chore,
PEG feed and tracheostomy care brings me
down to spoon 4.

During a seizure I dislocate my knee,
The convulsions and pain means I'm down to
spoon 3.

The pain triggers a reaction; an Epipen used,
Again another spoon down leaving me now with
just 2.

Yet another spoon used to put my pyjamas on,
I'm down to my final spoon, where on earth has
today gone?!

Forget the weekly food shop, forgot the bank
and bills,
My health is more important so I take note of
how I feel.

My body is exhausted, I feel the throbbing in my
head
The wisest decision I've made today
Is using my last spoon to climb into bed

*Inspired by 'the Spoon Theory' - Christine
Miserandino
www.butyoudontlooksick.com

Body & the Brain

I truly do believe that after years of being
constantly unwell and spending so much time in
hospital,
that our mind and body aren't separate.

I believe that mental and physical health
problems go hand in hand - physical illness is a
strain on your mind, and mental illness is a
strain on your body.

Unfortunately though, there is still a stigma
around mental health, an untruth that it's
something to be ashamed of.

It's this ignorance that means that so many
people suffer in silence and don't get offered the
help that is available.

This is a reminder to the chronically ill, that no
one should define themselves or be defined by
their medical condition(s).

You are more than your diagnosis.
You are more than the list of hospital
appointments on your calendar.

You are more than the multiple medications you take each day.
You are more than any aspect of your illness.

Still be strong, because "you never know how strong you are until being strong is the only choice you have".

And remember that before anything else, you are you, and no one can ever take that away from you.

COVID-19

Covid-nineteen,
An illness unseen
Which spread and plagued the world.

As quickly as it spread
We had no plans ahead
For the upcoming quarantine.

We were all in shock
As we watched the clock
For updates broadcast on the TV

Everyone was told
That until whilst these events unfold,
We must stay indoors all we can.

The only exception,
Given a different direction
Were those who worked in the sector of care.

The chronically ill,
Had it harder still,
With stricter instructions to shield.

This meant we couldn't see,

Our friends or family,
And necessities were brought directly to our
door.

They were working hard on an injection
To stop this infection
That was killing people all over the world.

They made us social distance,
In case of an instance,
Where an infected person passes it to the next.

I'm lucky to say,
That up until today,
COVID hasn't made its way to me yet!

Steroids (Prednisolone!)

Moon face
Weight gain
Fat deposits
Body pain

Poor vision
Always hot
Unexplained bruises
Acne spots

Broken bones
Fluid retention
Acid reflux
Indigestion

Unstable hormones
Adrenal suppression
Behavioural changes
Anxiety, depression

Late development
Poor concentration
Insomnia, restlessness
Procrastination

Intensive care; life & death

Mentally, being forced to adapt to a life where I
spend more time in hospital than at home,
Where the life-threatening nature of the
symptoms you suffer mean 999 is on speed dial
on your phone.

Where a diagnosis of Sepsis that you coped with
for as long as you could, lands you in ITU,
Only for the reason to keep you alive, so they
can throw every treatment they have at you.

But Intensive Care looks after the sickest of
them all and is not a place that you'd choose to
be,
A place where people of all ages are comatose
and most being kept alive by machines.

Seeing people of all ages take their last breath,
and couples arranging their marriage last minute,
the groom in his bed before his imminent death,
is not really the wedding you dream of, is it?

Witnessing both successful and unsuccessful
attempts at CPR by a 'Crash team' of
anaesthetists,

The defib detecting a 'shockable pulse',
sometimes lasting up to forty-five minutes.

Over-hearing conversations that Doctor's are
having with patients being forced to listen to the
painful truth,
News that no one wants to hear, let alone on a
ward, where Doctor's think that the curtains are
sound-proof.

Witnessing families being ripped apart by
heartbreak at the loss of their loved ones,
Seeing death in real life is so very different to
what is made for TV.

I've been put in situations that no one should
ever have to experience; let alone at the age of
16,
But I had no choice, I need to be there, in ITU,
so my monitors could always be seen.

And finally, the emotional impact that it had;
perhaps the hardest part of all,
Was seeing my friends climbing and reaching
milestones in life, whilst each step just caused
me to fall.

Intubation (Life Support)

I'll never forget when I was intubated
After being transferred from my local A&E,
A doctor came round, saw my swollen tongue,
And told me it was the safest thing for me.

With tears in my eyes, I was petrified,
So he took my hand in his,
"You'll be fine", he said, "we'll look after you",
And off to la la land I went.

I was scared of the anaesthetic,
I was scared how long I'd be asleep,
I was scared they wouldn't be able to wake me
up,
I was scared for my family to weep.

I was scared of what would happen,
I was scared of what they will find,
I was scared at the same time they'd find
nothing,
I was scared they'd think it's in my mind.

I was scared that first I'd stop breathing,
I was scared of what I'd hear and see,
I was scared of waking to tubes and lines,

I was scared that I wouldn't be me.

But I awoke to the faces of my family,
They reassured me that everything was fine,
I realised then that is the NHS we must thank,
For keeping people like me alive!

Hallucinations

There I was, laying quietly in bed,
Until I see pigeons flying round my head.
Upon further inspection they had covered the
ward too,
I screamed for help, what more could I do?

Next came red ants in my IV line,
I showed you the tube and you told me 'it was
fine',
You tried to reassure me that nothing was there,
I didn't know whether to believe you or if you
just didn't care.

I tried covering my eyes to block them out,
But all I could do is scream and shout,
The cobwebs that were in the corner was
covered in spiders eggs.
You ignored my plea to move them, but still I
begged and begged.

I couldn't cope when tarantulas started crawling
in my bed,
You ignored me and told me they were in my
head,

So when no one was looking, I headed for the door,
Pulling out my feeding tube as I fell to the floor.

After I complained about the venomous snake,
I could tell that I had another dose of meds to take,
As soon as you administered them all was gone again,
And I realised you were right, they were only in my brain!

Family

Thank you to my family
for always being there
You gave up your life when I got sick
Just to provide my care

And that you did, without a doubt,
I can't ever thank you enough
You've been my rock since the very first day
When things were really tough

Even when it was touch and go,
By my bedside you were sat
Watching my blood pressure, heart rate and
breathing
And monitoring my sats!

You've answered every single call,
When I'm sobbing and deflated
At any hour and every hour
You've made me less frustrated

Some times I feel so guilty
For all I've put you through,
But I'm proud of just how far I've come,
And that's all thanks to you.

Friends

It's hard to describe chronic illness
There is so much that I could say
It's not to be taken lightly;
No one is always okay.

But it also isn't all negative,
You can find something good in each day
If it weren't for the online community,
I wouldn't be the person I am today.

I've met the best friends I could wish for,
The people that genuinely care,
To now think of a life without them
Is a thought that I don't want to bear.

To the friends that I met in person,
At our worst on the hospital ward
It's fair to say that we've outweighed the bad
times
With more alcohol than we can even afford!

Those of you who I've met at a distance,
You're just as important to me,
Whether it be via support groups or otherwise,
You've become the best friends you could be.

So thank you for keeping life 'normal'
For only ever being at the end of the phone,
Without you in my life, (you know who you
are),
Where I'd be now we'll leave as unknown.

Carers

C is for compassionate, for calming, and co-operative

A is for accepting, for accommodating and attentive

R is for resilient, for respectful and responsive

E is for encouraging, for empowering and effective

R is for reliable, for rational and reactive, and

S is for sensational, sympathetic and supportive

Charities

Fundraising and donations
Are so incredibly important
For the charities that support us
With such a humble approach

The affect that they have
Is not one to be ignored
Because the support they provide
Is second to none

Whether you're looking for advice
Or you feel isolated and alone
There's always someone around
Who will make you feel more sane!

Charities create communities
Of like-minded people
That you can reach out to for help
And where strangers become friends

You can attend charity events
All are so sociable and friendly
It's not uncommon to feel overwhelmed
At the amount of people who understand you

So never underestimate
The power of charities
They need your support,
As much as you rely on theirs

My husband (Sam)

Who would have known
That from a blog that I own
I would find the love of my life?

Meeting through lockdown,
We never put the phone down!
It was enough for me to know he was the one.

Restrictions taken away,
We arranged to meet halfway,
And we both knew our future would be together.

Now we rent a flat
He proposed and after that,
We had the fairytale wedding day of our dreams

Your illness should not stop you
From doing anything you want to,
And we are living proof of that.

A poem written by Sam

My wife inspires me every day
I'm proud of her what can I say

She is kind, caring and thoughtful
Even when shes feeling awful

She helps others with poor health
Even with the bad cards she's be dealt

Her bravery is amazing
The path she takes is always sustaining

She shines like a light
And inspires me to fight

To me she's beautiful
That feeling is indisputable

I'll be her rock and best friend
Until the very end

That's a promise that'll never be broken.

Thank you

Thank you to all who have read my first book
It's full of all kinds of emotion if you take a
close look
For me this is just the start of sharing my
journey with you,
And I hope before long I'll be writing book two.

Milton Keynes UK
Ingram Content Group UK Ltd.
UKHW020938220424
441551UK00019B/1424

9 789358 313505